Contents

A hurricane strikes

"We grabbed a lady and pulled her out of the window, and then we swam with the current. It was terrifying. You should have seen the cars floating around us. We had to push them away when we were trying to swim." These were the words of a woman who lost her home when Hurricane Katrina hit the coast of the U.S.A. in August 2005.

Hurricane names
Weather experts have lists of names for hurricanes. They use a different list for each year. When a hurricane forms, it is given the next name on the list. If a hurricane is especially damaging, such as Katrina, its name is never used again.

Residents of New Orleans, Louisiana stand in the flooded streets in the days after Hurricane Katrina hit the city.

KINGFISHER
READERS

level
5

Hurricanes

Chris Oxlade

KINGFISHER
NEW YORK

KINGFISHER
LONDON & NEW YORK

Distributed in the U.S. and Canada by Macmillan, 175 Fifth Ave., New York, NY 10010

Library of Congress Cataloging-in-Publication data has been applied for.

Series editor: Thea Feldman
Literacy consultant: Ellie Costa, Bank Street College, New York
Hurricanes consultant: Dr. Pete Inness, Department of Meteorology, University of Reading, U.K.

ISBN: 978-0-7534-6963-7 (HB)
ISBN: 978-0-7534-6933-0 (PB)

Kingfisher books are available for special promotions
and premiums. For details contact: Special Markets
Department, Macmillan, 175 Fifth Ave., New York, NY 10010.

For more information, please visit www.kingfisherbooks.com

Printed in China
9 8 7 6 5 4 3 2 1
1TR/1012/WKT/UG/105MA

Picture credits

The Publisher would like to thank the following for permission to reproduce their material. Every care has been taken to trace copyright holders. However, if there have been unintentional omissions or failure to trace copyright holders, we apologize and will, if informed, endeavor to make corrections in any future edition.
(t = top; b = bottom; c = center; r = right; l = left): Cover Shutterstock (SS)/B747, Alamy/Marvin Dembinsky, Kingfisher Archive/Mark Bergin, Corbis/China Newsphoto; 2cl Getty/Mark Wilson; 2c Corbis/Mike Theiss/Ultimate Chase; 2cr Corbis/Alberto Garcia; 2r Getty/MC1 Brandon Schulze; 3l Corbis/Eduardo Munoz/Reuters; 3c Getty/James Nielsen; 3cr Corbis/Michael Ainsworth; 3r Corbis/Bettman; 4 Getty/Mark Wilson; 5t Corbis/Mona Reeder; 5b Corbis/U.S. Air Force; 6t Getty/Stocktrek Images; 6–7 Getty/Mike Theiss/NGS; 8 Corbis/Imaginechina; 9cr Getty/Mark Wilson; 9b Corbis/Steve Brennan/epa; 10 all NASA/Visible Earth; 13b Alamy/Marvin Dembinsky; 15t Corbis/NOAA/Zuma; 15b Corbis/NOAA; 16 Corbis/China Newsphoto; 17t Corbis/Mike Theiss/Ultimate Chase; 18 Getty/AFP; 19t Corbis/Smiley N. Pool; 19b Alamy/Mary Evans Picture Library; 20 Corbis; 21b Corbis/Reuters; 22t Corbis/Henry Romero/Reuters; 22b Corbis/Henry Romero/Reuters; 23 Corbis/Imaginechina; 24 Corbis/Imaginechina; 25t Corbis/Imaginechina; 25b Corbis/Imaginechina; 26 Corbis/Alberto Garcia; 27 Corbis/Yann-Arthus Bertrand; 28 Alamy/Kevin Howchin; 29t Corbis/Jim Reed/Science Faction; 29b SS/Mamut Vision; 30 Getty/James Nielsen; 31 Corbis/U.S. Coastguard; 32t Corbis/David Bathgate; 33t Getty/Mehdi Fedouach; 33b Getty/MC1 Brandon Schulze; 34 Getty/Erik Simonsen; 35t Corbis/Ed Darack; 35b Corbis/Jim Edds; 36–37 Alamy/David R. Frazier; 37t Alamy/Ilene MacDonald; 38cl Getty/Joe Raedle; 38–39 Corbis/Tim Johnson; 39t Corbis/Michael Ainsworth; 40 Corbis/David Gard; 41t Getty/David McNew; 41b Corbis/Seaman Ash Severe U.S. Navy; 42tl Corbis/Tannen Maury/epa; 42c Getty/Fox Photos; 42bl Alamy/Borderlands; 43tl Corbis/Reuters; 43b Corbis/Bettman; 44t Getty/AFP; 44–45 Alamy/Jim West; 42 Corbis/Pedro Ultreras/Demotix; 46l Getty/Mark Wilson; 46cl Corbis/Mike Theiss/Ultimate Chase; 46cr Corbis/Alberto Garcia; 46r Getty/MC1 Brandon Schulze; 47l Corbis/Eduardo Munoz/Reuters; 47c Getty/James Nielsen; 47cr Corbis/Michael Ainsworth; 47r Corbis/Bettman

A New Orleans resident paddles a boat through the flooded streets near his home.

Hurricane Katrina caused terrible **floods** in the city of New Orleans. The city is protected from the sea by walls and earth banks, called **levees**. When Hurricane Katrina hit, **sea levels** rose so high that water spilled over these levees. Three-quarters of the city was flooded by water, with only the roofs of houses left showing. Thousands of people in the city didn't want to leave their homes or thought that they were safe. Sadly, more than 1,800 people died.

A member of a U.S. Air Force rescue team looks for survivors in the flooded streets of New Orleans.

What is a hurricane?

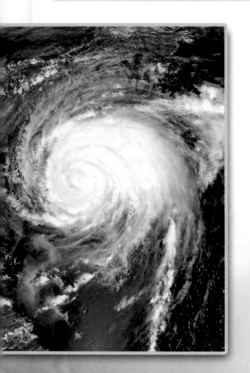

A hurricane is a giant, spinning **storm**. A hurricane can be hundreds of miles across and more than 6 miles (10 kilometers) high. Inside a hurricane are thick clouds, **thunderstorms**, and heavy rain. There are also superstrong winds, which can blow at more than 150 mph (250km/h).

This photograph was taken by a **satellite** in space. It shows the swirling clouds of a hurricane, seen from above.

A hurricane's strong winds create huge waves at sea. They also push up the surface of the sea into a bulge, called a **storm surge**. If a hurricane hits land, the winds wreck buildings and the storm surge floods the coast. A hurricane's heavy rain can also cause flooding.

Hurricane is the word for a huge storm in the Atlantic Ocean. In some parts of the world, hurricanes are called **typhoons**. In other places, they are called **cyclones**.

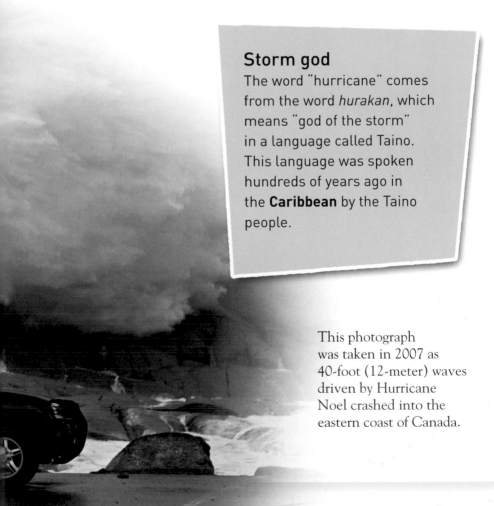

Storm god
The word "hurricane" comes from the word *hurakan*, which means "god of the storm" in a language called Taino. This language was spoken hundreds of years ago in the **Caribbean** by the Taino people.

This photograph was taken in 2007 as 40-foot (12-meter) waves driven by Hurricane Noel crashed into the eastern coast of Canada.

Where and when?

Hurricanes only happen in some parts of the world, and they only happen during certain months of the year. The time of year when hurricanes form is called the **hurricane season**. In the Atlantic Ocean, the hurricane season lasts from June to November.

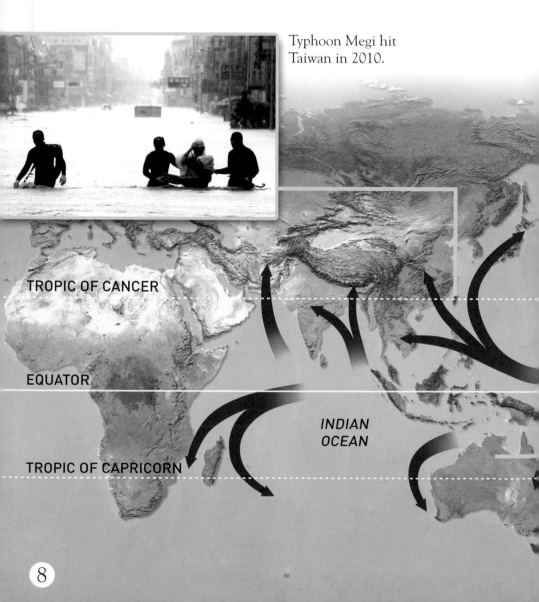

Typhoon Megi hit
Taiwan in 2010.

TROPIC OF CANCER

EQUATOR

INDIAN
OCEAN

TROPIC OF CAPRICORN

Hurricanes only happen in an area of the world called the **tropics**. This area is like a wide belt around the middle of the world. It includes the land and sea on both sides of the **equator**.

The map below shows the places in the world where hurricanes happen. The arrows show where hurricanes start, near the equator, the paths they follow across the sea, and where they hit land.

Hurricane Katrina struck the southeastern U.S.A. in 2005.

PACIFIC OCEAN

ATLANTIC OCEAN

Cyclone Larry struck northern Australia in 2006.

The life cycle of a hurricane

Every hurricane has a **life cycle**. It forms, grows in size, moves across the ocean for a few days or weeks, and then fades away.

1. A hurricane always starts life as a thunderstorm over a warm sea.

2. A group of thunderstorms sometimes turns into a spinning storm, called a **tropical storm**.

3. A tropical storm grows bigger and its wind speeds increase. Eventually, when the winds are fast enough, it becomes a hurricane.

4. When a hurricane moves over land, or over cooler sea, it gets less energy. It slowly gets weaker, and its winds die down. Eventually, it dies away.

Katrina's life cycle

Hurricane Katrina began near the Bahamas, on August 23, 2005. For a few days, it was fairly weak. But it grew much stronger as it moved over the warm waters of the Gulf of Mexico. It finally died out at the end of August, over the south of the United States.

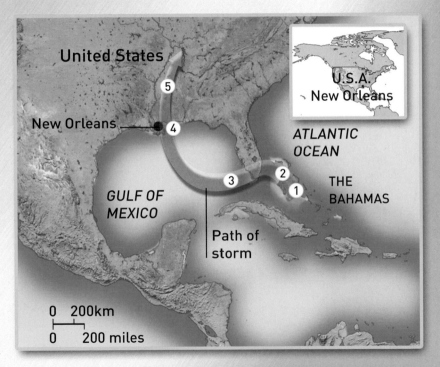

1. August 23: Katrina starts as a group of thunderstorms.
2. August 24: Katrina becomes a tropical storm.
3. August 27: Katrina becomes a hurricane.
4. August 29: Hurricane Katrina moves over New Orleans.
5. August 30: the hurricane becomes a tropical storm and begins to die away.

How hurricanes begin

All hurricanes begin over warm seas near the equator. There, the weather is always hot. Water **evaporates** from the warm sea and turns into **water vapor** in the warm air. The warm air floats upward and then cools off. When it cools, the water vapor turns back into liquid water and forms millions of tiny drops. These drops make up clouds. The clouds grow thicker and taller, until they are huge **thunderclouds** more than 6 miles (10 kilometers) high.

1. A group of thunderstorms forms over tropical land or sea.

2. The storms pull warm air upward, creating low pressure on the surface of the ocean.

How many hurricanes?
On average, there are 85 hurricanes and other tropical storms every year. Most of them are only small storms, and many die out before they reach any land.

3. The spinning of Earth causes the storm to rotate.

Thunderstorms are very common in the warm, moist air of the tropics.

Sometimes a group of thunderstorms begins to spin slowly. This happens because Earth itself is spinning. They become a giant swirling storm, called a tropical storm. Many tropical storms die away, but some get stronger and stronger. When the wind inside a tropical storm blows at more than 73 mph (118km/h), the storm is officially a hurricane.

This is a tropical storm called Alberto, which formed in the Caribbean Sea in 2006.

The structure of a hurricane

Hurricanes are made up of bands of clouds spinning around a central point. They can grow to be truly enormous, with some hurricanes reaching hundreds of miles from one side to the other.

Right in the middle of a hurricane there is a round hole with no cloud. This is called the eye. If you were standing under the eye of a hurricane, you would see blue sky above you.

This diagram of a hurricane shows the eye in the middle surrounded by bands of cloud.

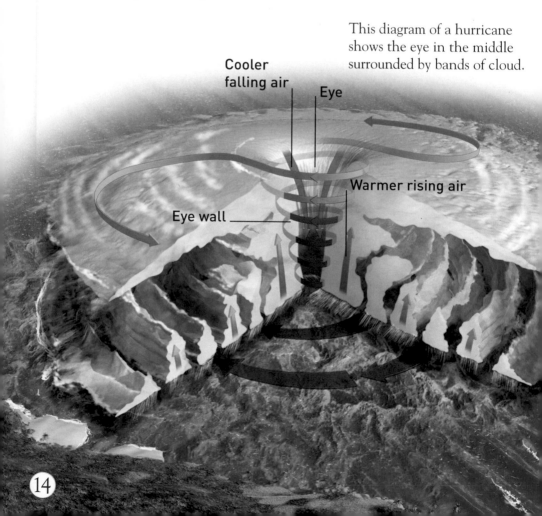

Cooler falling air

Eye

Warmer rising air

Eye wall

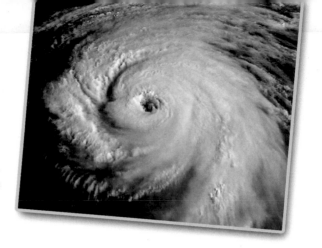

This satellite photo of Hurricane Katrina clearly shows the eye in the center.

Normally the eye is about 30 miles (50 kilometers) across, but it can be as small as 6 miles (10 kilometers) or as large as 125 miles (200 kilometers) across.

Around the eye is a bank of tall clouds, known as the eye wall. This is where the strongest winds blow. In the eye itself the winds are calm.

The eye wall of Hurricane Katrina seen from a plane.

Hurricane winds

Hurricanes bring very strong winds. Even the weakest hurricanes have winds blowing at more than 73 mph (118km/h). That means the air is moving as fast as a car traveling on a highway. More powerful hurricanes have winds reaching average speeds of more than 155 mph (250km/h), which is as fast as a high-speed train.

Thunderstorms around the eye of a hurricane can cause **tornadoes**. These can bring even stronger winds, blowing at up to 250 mph (500km/h).

People in eastern China struggle to stay upright in the fierce winds of Typhoon Haitang, in 2005.

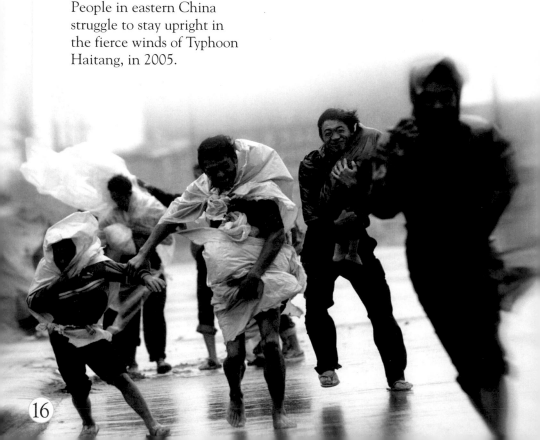

16

As a hurricane approaches, the winds get stronger and stronger. But as the hurricane's eye passes overhead, the winds die away. This often makes people think that the hurricane is gone, but then the winds get stronger again and blow even more fiercely than before.

This aircraft was tossed into a tree by hurricane winds.

Measuring hurricanes

Weather experts grade hurricanes from 1 to 5, according to their wind speed. A Category-1 storm causes flooding and moderate damage. A Category-5 storm causes almost total destruction.

Category 1: wind speed 74–95 mph (119–153km/h)
Category 2: wind speed 96–110mph (154–177km/h)
Category 3: wind speed 111–129 mph (178–208km/h)
Category 4: wind speed 130–156 mph (209–251km/h)
Category 5: wind speed over 157 mph (252km/h)

Wind damage

A hurricane's winds whip up big waves at sea and cause a lot of damage when they hit land. When a hurricane's strong winds blow across the surface of the sea, they make waves. As the winds get stronger, the waves get bigger. The waves can be more than 82 feet (25 meters) high. That's as high as a seven-story building. Waves this big can overturn and sink small boats and damage big ships and oil platforms.

This boat was damaged when Hurricane Jimena hit the west coast of Mexico, in 2009.

When a hurricane hits land, the winds make a terrible screaming noise, knocking down trees and telegraph poles and ripping pieces off buildings. Debris, such as tree branches, roof tiles, street signs, and garden furniture, flies around in the streets.

Winds from Hurricane Ivan caused this wall to fall into the street in Florida, in 2004.

Divine winds

In the 1200s, Kublai Khan, the ruler of Mongolia, tried to invade Japan from huge fleets of ships, but the ships were hit by typhoons and badly damaged. The Japanese thought that their gods had sent the typhoons to protect them, so they called the typhoons *Kamikaze*, (say "Kah-mik-**ah**-zee") which means "divine wind."

Hurricane Andrew

In August 1992, Hurricane Andrew hit Florida. Its winds caused terrible damage in the city of Miami.

Hurricane Andrew began on August 17 as a tropical storm in the middle of the Atlantic Ocean. At first, its winds were not very strong and weather forecasters were not too worried. But on August 22, its winds got stronger. It grew bigger and stronger so quickly that by the next day it was a Category-5 hurricane, bringing winds with speeds of more than 150 mph (240km/h).

This combination of three satellite photographs shows how Hurricane Andrew moved across Florida.

"I was hiding in the closet. I'm telling you, I'm never living through one of those things again. I was just scared to death, scared to death, scared to death."

—Jim Bossick, who was caught in Hurricane Andrew

A person struggles to walk in the winds of Hurricane Andrew.

Then, in the early hours of Monday, August 24, Hurricane Andrew hit Florida. The eye of the hurricane passed straight over the city of Miami. More than 20,000 mobile homes and other buildings were wrecked by gusts of wind blowing at more than 200 mph (320km/h). In all, 61 people were killed.

Hurricane Andrew's winds lifted this heavy truck into the air and then dropped it on a building.

Rain and floods

A hurricane carries billions of tons of water in its clouds. The water comes from the sea. It evaporates from the sea and forms drops of water that make up the clouds. When the hurricane moves over land, most of this water falls back to the ground as rain.

Heavy rain, dropped by Hurricane Wilma in 2005, caused floods in Mexico.

When the heavy rain from a hurricane hits the ground, it quickly fills streams and rivers, which can overflow in minutes, flooding the land on either side. These floods are called **flash floods**.

A flash flood in Haiti, caused by rainfall from tropical storm Alpha in 2005, destroyed many houses.

Rescue workers search the flooded streets of a city in Taiwan after Typhoon Megi struck the country in 2010.

Floodwater fills the streets with dirty water. It stops drains and sewers from working correctly. Sometimes there is no clean water left to drink, which means that diseases can spread.

Typhoon Morakot

In 2009, torrential rain from Typhoon Morakot caused disastrous floods in Taiwan. The typhoon took a day to cross Taiwan. Its winds were not very strong, but the rain was very intense. Enough rain fell to cover the ground with water that was 9 feet (2.8 meters) deep in places.

Floods and **mudslides** washed away mountain villages, destroyed bridges and roads, and trapped thousands of people. The village of Hsiaolin (say "Sh-ow-lin") was wiped out by a **landslide** of soaking wet earth. In total, more than 500 people in Taiwan were killed as a result of Typhoon Morakot.

Rain from Typhoon Morakot made this river swell into a powerful torrent, causing buildings on the bank to collapse.

"Standing at the spot where Hsiaolin village used to be, I could not see any man-made object: no building wreckage, no car parts, and no articles for daily use. All I saw were huge rocks, mud, and driftwood."

—Resident of Hsiaolin village, Taiwan

After Taiwan, Typhoon Morakot moved on to China, where about one million people were evacuated as it approached. It caused even more destruction, before slowly dying away.

A flooded street in China after Typhoon Morakot.

Mudslides on Pinatubo

In the Philippines in 1991, a **volcano** called Mount Pinatubo erupted at the same time as a typhoon called Yunya arrived. Ash from the volcano mixed with rain from the typhoon, creating deadly mudslides.

Giant ash flows smothered the fields around Pinatubo in 1991.

First, Mount Pinatubo erupted with giant explosions. Millions of tons of ash were blasted high up into the air. The ash settled all over the volcano's sides and on the land around the volcano.

Then Typhoon Yunya arrived. Heavy rain from its giant clouds mixed with ash on the ground, making thick, heavy mud. The mud flowed quickly down the volcano's slopes. It swept across farmland and into towns and villages. When the mud stopped, it set like concrete, trapping everything in it. Most people had moved to safety because of the eruption, but their homes and crops were destroyed.

Quick mud

The mudslides that flowed from Mount Pinatubo reached speeds of 40 mph (65km/h). Some flowed 50 miles (80 kilometers) before they stopped.

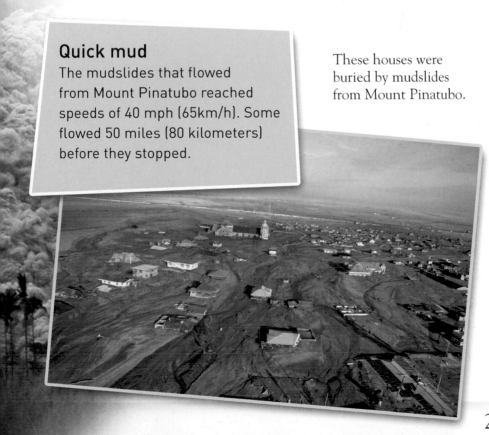

These houses were buried by mudslides from Mount Pinatubo.

Storm surges

As a hurricane moves across the sea, its winds push the water on the surface ahead of it. This makes a mound of water called a storm surge. A hurricane sucks the sea's surface upward a little, making the storm surge higher still. A powerful hurricane can create a storm surge several feet high.

A hurricane's storm surge often does more damage than its winds and rain. If a hurricane reaches the shore, its storm surge raises the sea level at the shore. If the storm surge is high enough, the sea flows across the land at the coast. The water can flow many miles inland.

This storm surge has rushed up the Saint Lawrence river in Quebec, Canada.

A yacht lies in a parking lot near Fort Pierce, Florida. It was carried there by the storm surge of Hurricane Frances, in September 2004.

Huge waves created by the hurricane's winds can sweep inland, too, making the flooding worse. A storm surge wrecks buildings on the coast and carries boats and ships inland.

Animal dangers
During a storm surge, people caught in the water can be bitten by panic-stricken animals such as snakes and alligators.

Katrina's storm surge

By the time Hurricane Katrina hit the south coast of the United States, its storm surge had grown to nearly 30 feet (9 meters) high. The surge caused seawater to flood into towns and cities along the south coast of the United States, including New Orleans, Louisiana.

New Orleans lies on the Mississippi River and is next to a lake connected to the sea. As Katrina approached, its storm surge made the sea level rise. This made the level of water in the Mississippi and the lake rise, too. Eventually, water started flowing into the city.

A man is pulled from his home by rescue workers in a boat on the day that Hurricane Katrina hit New Orleans.

The people of New Orleans were warned, but thousands of them decided to stay. Many people got stuck inside their houses and had to wait for days to be rescued. Along the coast, the nearby cities of Gulfport and Biloxi were badly damaged, as water from the storm surge rushed ashore.

Many roads in New Orleans became completely submerged in floodwater.

"My town is gone. The winds and waves have taken a once-great beachside town and totally washed it away."

—Resident of Gulfport

Cyclones in Bangladesh

Bangladesh is a country in Asia. It has suffered many terrible disasters because of cyclones.

This is typical low-lying farmland in Bangladesh.

A lot of the countryside in Bangladesh is flat and only a few feet above the level of the sea. Along the coast there are many islands. Millions of people live in these low-lying areas. Most of these people are poor farmers, who live in simple homes made from mud and straw.

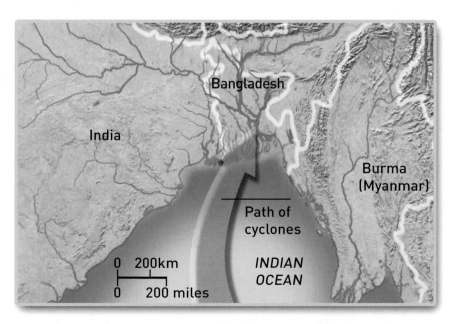

This map shows the route that cyclones normally take through the Indian Ocean as they approach Bangladesh.

Cyclone Sidr

Cyclone Sidr hit the coast of Bangladesh on November 15, 2007, with wind speeds up to 160 mph (260km/h) and a storm surge 16 feet (5 meters) high. Buildings along the coast were flattened, and cities, including the capital Dhaka, were badly flooded. Almost 3,500 people lost their lives, and half a million people lost their homes.

Cyclones often start their life cycles in the Indian Ocean, which is south of Bangladesh, and move north. Sometimes they hit the coast of Bangladesh. The storm surges from these cyclones sweep across the land, washing away homes and leaving fields under water.

Hurricane spotters

About one-eighth of all the people in the world live in places where hurricanes can strike. They need to know if a hurricane is coming so that they can get prepared or leave their homes. Expert **weather forecasters** watch out for new hurricanes all the time.

The forecasters look out for new tropical storms beginning over the ocean. Then they watch them to see if they grow into hurricanes. They watch how fast hurricanes move and which way they are going using photographs taken by satellites in space. They also measure how fast the winds in hurricanes are blowing.

Weather satellites allow forecasters
to watch the movements of hurricanes.

Flying through the eye of a hurricane

Sometimes special planes, called **hurricane hunters**, fly right into hurricanes to measure the winds, the temperature of the air, and other things about the hurricane. They also take photographs.

Into the storm
Most pilots avoid flying into storms because they get a very bumpy ride, but hurricane hunters fly right through hurricanes!

Making predictions

When weather forecasters have all the information that they need about a hurricane, they try to predict what the hurricane will do next.

All the information that forecasters have about a hurricane—its size and speed, as well as the strength of its winds, is fed into a powerful computer. The computer figures out what might happen to the hurricane next—whether it will get stronger or weaker and which way it will go. The forecasters also try to figure out how high a hurricane's storm surge will be when it hits land.

Regular weather updates are broadcast on
television when hurricanes are approaching.

When a hurricane approaches land, forecasters give
out hurricane warnings on television, radio, and the
Internet. The warnings are issued to try to make sure
that people are ready if the hurricane does arrive.

Which way?
Hurricanes are fairly
unpredictable, and they can
change direction suddenly.
This makes it difficult for
forecasters to say exactly
when and where a hurricane
will hit land until a day or so
before it actually does.

A weather forecaster examines
satellite images and weather
data, which he will use to help
make a forecast.

37

Preparing for a hurricane

When people know that a hurricane is coming, they can prepare for its arrival. The first thing that people need is a hurricane survival kit. This contains all the things that they might need during a hurricane. A survival kit might contain food in cans, bottles of drinking water, a camping stove and pans, spare clothes, a first-aid kit, a flashlight, and a radio. Stores often stock extra supplies of these items, ready to sell when a hurricane is on its way.

Shopping for emergency supplies

These men are boarding up windows in New Orleans before the arrival of Hurricane Katrina in 2005.

People need to protect their homes and property during a hurricane. They need to put loose objects, such as garden furniture, indoors, to stop them from blowing around and causing damage. They also need to cover windows and doors with boards, to stop the windows from breaking.

If forecasters are expecting a big storm surge, people need to leave their homes because there could be dangerous flooding. In big cities, millions of people may need to leave. There are normally special **evacuation** routes for people to follow in their cars. People without cars may be evacuated in buses or by train.

A line of school buses evacuates citizens of Galveston, Texas before the arrival of Hurricane Rita in 2005.

Surviving a hurricane

As a hurricane approaches land, people need to find a **storm shelter**, in order to stay safe from strong winds and flying debris. Some homes have their own storm shelters. There are also public storm shelters where people can go. These are often in local schools or sports centers.

Slowly, the hurricane moves past. After a few hours, the winds begin to die down. Floodwater slowly flows away as the sea level falls again and the rain stops.

Temporary beds in the Louisiana Superdome, in New Orleans. This was the main hurricane shelter during Hurricane Katrina, in 2005.

These temporary houses are being quickly constructed for people left without homes after Hurricane Katrina.

Once the hurricane is gone, it's time to clean up. Floodwater needs to be pumped away, debris needs to be cleared from the streets, and buildings need to be repaired. The many people who have lost their homes in the hurricane need help to rebuild their homes and communities. Poorer countries sometimes need **aid** from other countries.

Emergency supplies from the U.S. arrive in Bangladesh for the victims of Cyclone Sidr, in 2007.

The worst hurricanes

Below are some of the worst hurricanes, cyclones, and typhoons that have happened in the world over the last 100 years.

1. Hurricane Katrina, 2005
This was the hurricane that did the most damage in the U.S. It cost between $100 to $200 billion to repair the damage.

2. Galveston hurricane of 1900
This was the deadliest hurricane to hit the U.S. It was a Category-4 hurricane that hit the city of Galveston, Texas. Its storm surge washed right over the city, killing between 6,000 and 12,000 people.

3. Hurricane Mitch, 1998
This was the deadliest hurricane ever in the Atlantic Ocean. It killed about 18,000 people in the countries of Central America. Many people died in mudslides.

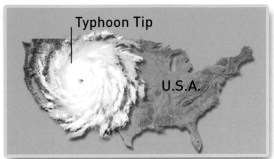

Typhoon Tip

U.S.A.

4. Great Labor Day Storm, 1935
This was the most powerful hurricane to hit the U.S. It was a Category-5 hurricane that caused 423 deaths in Florida.

5. Typhoon Tip, 1979
This was the biggest ever tropical storm. It formed in the Pacific Ocean. At one point, Typhoon Tip was over 1,400 miles (2,200 kilometers) across, which is about half the width of the U.S.A.

6. Bhola Cyclone, 1970
This was the deadliest storm ever recorded, anywhere in the world. The cyclone swept into Bangladesh and killed more than 500,000 people.

Predict to prepare

This hurricane forecaster in the Philippines points to a satellite image of Typhoon Lupit, in 2009.

One hundred years ago, people did not understand hurricanes. They didn't know a hurricane was coming until it arrived. Today, weather forecasters can see hurricanes coming days in advance. They try to predict when and where hurricanes will hit land, so that people can be warned.

Today, we can also deal with the dangers of hurricanes better. In places where hurricanes are common, people have action plans for when hurricanes are coming. There are organized evacuation routes, hurricane shelters, hurricane-proof hospitals, and **flood defenses** against storm surges.

We know much more about hurricanes, but we can still improve the way in which we protect ourselves from them. In 2005, Hurricane Katrina showed that even wealthy modern cities can still be badly hit by severe hurricanes.

New homes like this one, in New Orleans, were built on stilts after Hurricane Katrina in order to reduce the risk of damage from storm surges in the future.

A sign to a hurricane shelter, printed in different languages, in New York City, in preparation for Hurricane Irene, which hit the city in August 2011.

Glossary

aid help—for example, help given to a country after a disaster, including emergency supplies such as food and money

Caribbean the area of sea and the islands to the southeast of the United States

cyclones the name given to hurricanes in the Indian Ocean

equator an imaginary line around the middle of Earth, the same distance from each of Earth's poles

evacuation moving people away from danger

evaporates turns from a liquid into a gas

flash floods sudden floods that happen when intense rain makes a river burst its banks

floods when water from a river or the sea flows over land that is normally dry

flood defenses walls, banks, or other barriers, designed to stop water from flooding an area; a levee is a type of flood defense

floodwater water that has flooded over normally dry land

hurricane hunters aircraft that fly into a hurricane to allow scientists onboard to observe the hurricane's strength and growth

hurricane season the time of year when most hurricanes happen in a place

landslide when a hillside collapses, and earth and rock slide downward

levees types of flood defenses, or raised structures, that are built to prevent flooding

life cycle a series of stages through which something passes during its lifetime

mudslides mud that flows down a river or valley at high speed

satellite a spacecraft that is launched into space and orbits around Earth

sea levels the average levels of the seas' surfaces

storm a combination of strong winds and heavy rain or snow

storm shelter a strong building where people go for safety during a hurricane or other storm

storm surge the increase in sea level caused by a hurricane, which often causes flooding when a hurricane reaches land

thunderclouds clouds that bring heavy rain, lightning, and thunder

thunderstorms storms with lightning and thunder

tornadoes spinning columns of air that sometimes form over land, under a huge thunderstorm

tropical storm an intense storm that forms in the tropics and sometimes grows into a hurricane

tropics a hot region of the world on both sides of the equator

typhoons the name given to hurricanes in the Pacific Ocean

volcano a place where hot, molten rock comes out of Earth's surface

water vapor the gas form of water

weather forecasters scientists who predict what the weather will be like

Index